For The Good

GOD'S got this...

Thy Will be Done

HAVE FAITH

faith

Jesus is my calm

For The Good

TRUST IN THE LORD WITH ALL YOUR HEART

Thy Will be Done

HE HAS A PLAN I HAVE A PURPOSE

faith

Faithful Servant

MW00776718

Creative Christian

Sticker Inspirations

PRAISE AND PROMISES TO REMIND YOU OF GOD'S LOVE

Andrews McMeel
PUBLISHING®

choose
joy

LOVE

Faith > Fear

EVERY DAY IS A GOOD DAY
FOR JESUS

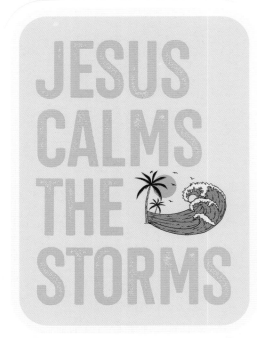

JESUS CALMS THE STORMS

We have this hope as an anchor for the soul, firm and secure.

-HEBREWS 6:19A (NIV)

"I tell you the truth, if you had faith even as small as a mustard seed, you could say to this mountain, 'Move from here to there,' and it would move. Nothing would be impossible."

—MATTHEW 17:20B (NLT)

A little caffeine, a lot of Christ

I RUN ON JESUS AND COFFEE

Be strong in faith

drink IN the good

FILL MY CUP Lord

No Longer Lost

LIGHT MY WAY

the Lord is my light

Bright Light, big God

Shine

Shine Jesus Shine

Waymaker out of the dark

I can do all things through Christ, who strengthens me.

—PHILIPPIANS 4:13 (WEB)

You make my lamp
bright. The Lord
my God lights
my darkness.

—PSALM 18:28 (NLV)

Rooted in christ

Hang on to God

Growing in grace

Bloom WHERE GOD PLANTS YOU

NURTURE FAITH

Just Trust

CONSIDER HOW · THE WILD FLOWERS GROW ·

Pray more Worry Less

Let go & let God

Have your roots planted deep in Christ. Grow in Him. Get your strength from Him. Let Him make you strong in the faith as you have been taught. Your life should be full of thanks to Him.

-COLOSSIANS 2:7 (NLV)

"Consider how the wild flowers grow. They do not labor or spin. Yet I tell you, not even Solomon in all his splendor was dressed like one of these."

–LUKE 12:27 (NIV)

He walks with me

Kingdom Goals

SEEK HIM FIRST

Jesus vibes

Trust & Obey

pray

**Seek the Kingdom of
God above all else,
and live righteously,
and he will give you
everything you need.**

–MATTHEW 6:33 (NLT)

And this is the boldness we have in him, that if we ask anything according to his will, he hears us.

–1 JOHN 5:14 (NRSVUE)

roll *with* **faith**

go with *god*

faith is alive

IF THE STARS WERE MADE TO WORSHIP SO WILL I

Shine

WHY WISH UPON A STAR WHEN YOU CAN PRAY TO GOD WHO CREATED THEM ALL?

Praise Him

Raise A Hallelujah

SHINING FOR GOD

But someone will say, "You have faith; I have deeds." Show me your faith without deeds, and I will show you my faith by my deeds.

–James 2:18 (NIV)

Praise Him, sun and moon! Praise Him, all you shining stars!

Praise Him, you highest heavens, and you waters above the heavens!

-PSALM 148:3-4 (NLV)

NOT today Satan

love

TEAM JESUS

GOD IS GOOD

His is the victory

GOD is for ME

Fully known, fully loved

god gets me

Behind & before

LOVE

God makes no mistakes

Wonderfully made

Since God is for us, who can be against us?

Who can keep us away from the love of Christ?

-ROMANS 8:31B, 35A (NLV)

I praise you, for I
am fearfully and
wonderfully made.

Wonderful are
your works; that I
know very well.

—PSALM 139:14 (NRSVUE)

peace

LOVE LEADS THE WAY

L♥VE LIKE JESUS

Righteous VIBES

Gather the good

PEACE PLANTER

Sing and Make Music from your Heart to the Lord

mourning to dancing

LOUD FOR
THE LORD

mercy & music

Jesus is My Song

PRAISE ON REPEAT

**Those who plant seeds
of peace will gather
what is right and good.**

−JAMES 3:18 (NLV)

Sing and make music from your heart to the Lord, always giving thanks to God the Father for everything, in the name of our Lord Jesus Christ.

–EPHESIANS 5:19B–20 (NIV)

RENEW YOUR MIND

Head in God's Clouds

Transformed

GOD'S WAY IS >

in the world, not of it

ALL WILL SEE

Bright and *Beautiful* with God

FOCUS on GOD

Can't hide my heart for Jesus

Glorify

BE THE LIGHT

Don't be conformed
to this world, but
be transformed
by the renewing
of your mind, so
that you may prove
what is the good,
well-pleasing, and
perfect will of God.

—ROMANS 12:2 (WEB)

Let your light shine
before others, so
that they may see
your good works and
give glory to your
Father in heaven.

–MATTHEW 5:16 (NRSVUE)

AMAZING Race, AMAZING Grace

Hustle HARD ✝ Pray HARDER

MY PRIZE is MY GOD

JESUS Always Only

thankful. grateful. blessed.

Every gift.
all the time ^

GOD IS GOOD

Life changes.
God does not.

Blessed

His promises
are true

And let us run with endurance the race God has set before us. We do this by keeping our eyes on Jesus, the champion who initiates and perfects our faith.

-HEBREWS 12:1B-2A (NLT)

Every good and perfect gift is from above, coming down from the Father of the heavenly lights, who does not change like shifting shadows.

–James 1:17 (NIV)

NEED A GOOD BOOK?

I TRUST THE NEXT CHAPTER BECAUSE I KNOW THE AUTHOR

THIS IS MY STORY, THIS IS MY SONG

God reads my heart

Spoiler Alert: God wins

Still I Will Say

Worthy to be praised

Rise and Shine

FROM SUNDOWN TO SON UP

Blessed
BE YOUR
NAME

For it became him, for whom are all things, and through whom are all things, in bringing many children to glory, to make the author of their salvation perfect through sufferings.

–HEBREWS 2:10 (WEB)

Blessed be the name of the Lord **from this time on and forevermore. From the rising of the sun to its setting, the name of the L**ord **is to be praised.**

—PSALM 113:2-3 (NRSVUE)

HOW **Deep** IS YOUR **Love**

WADING + DEEP FAITH, NO

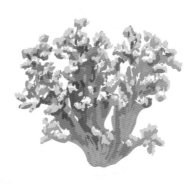

GRATEFUL FOR THE OCEAN FLOOR

GRACE UPON GRACE

WAVES of MERCY

for such a time as this

HE HAS A PLAN I HAVE A PURPOSE

Kingdom Come

you are here

Created with a Purpose

Once again you will have compassion on us. You will trample our sins under your feet and throw them into the depths of the ocean!

–MICAH 7:19 (NLT)

"Who knows if you haven't come to the kingdom for such a time as this?"

-ESTHER 4:14B (WEB)

Free INDEED

my
chains
are
gone

GRACE

Walk with GOD

Faithful Servant

GOD'S
LOVE
CHANGES
EVERYTHING

love

STAY HUMBLE

love MERCY

**So if the Son makes
you free, you will
be free indeed.**

–JOHN 8:36 (NRSVUE)

And what does
the LORD require of
you? To act justly
and to love mercy
and to walk humbly
with your God.

–MICAH 6:8B (NIV)

Where you go, He goes

Stand Strong in *faith*

God is in control

courageous in *Christ*

Be Strong

STAND FIRM IN THE FAITH

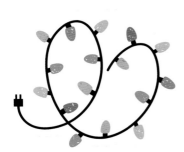

Power in love

LOVE NEVER fails

LOVE

Do Everything in Love

"Be strong and courageous; do not be frightened or dismayed, for the Lord your God is with you wherever you go."

—Joshua 1:9b (NRSVue)

Be on your guard;
stand firm in the faith;
be courageous; be strong.
Do everything in love.

–1 CORINTHIANS 16:13–14 (NIV)

I'M JUST OUT HERE TRUSTING GOD

The only perfect timing is God's

HE IS WORKING IN THE WAITING

just trust

GOD is Good all the Time

God's plan > my plan

Redeemed
Restored
Renewed

Chosen & called

NEVER IN
OVER MY
HEAD WITH
MY GOD

Redeemed

WATERPROOFED

He will
make
a way

BY GOD

N
W
E
S

"For I know the plans I have for you," declares the Lord, "plans to prosper you and not to harm you, plans to give you hope and a future."

–Jeremiah 29:11 (NIV)

"Do not fear, for I have redeemed you;
I have summoned you by
name; you are mine.
When you pass through the waters,
I will be with you;
and when you pass
through the rivers,
they will not sweep over you."

–ISAIAH 43:1B–2A (NIV)

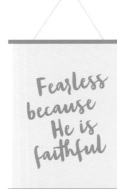

Fearless because He is faithful

Fear ends where faith begins

It is well

WHEN IN DOUBT, PRAY IT OUT

know Jesus, know Peace

PEACE

Peace

god vibes

faith

Look up

ALL THE LOVELY THINGS

JESUS

choose

peace

hope

faith

"Peace I leave with you; my peace I give you. I do not give to you as the world gives. Do not let your hearts be troubled and do not be afraid."

–JOHN 14:27 (NIV)

Finally, brothers and sisters, whatever is true, whatever is noble, whatever is right, whatever is pure, whatever is lovely, whatever is admirable— if anything is excellent or praiseworthy—think about such things.

—PHILIPPIANS 4:8 (NIV)

JESUS is the WAY

Made new in Christ

THE PAST IS FORGOTTEN

[BORN]²

Redemption > regrets

Limitless

LOVE

Power
in the Blood

Jesus So Loved

HE is GREATER

Therefore, if anyone is in Christ, the new creation has come: The old has gone, the new is here!

–2 CORINTHIANS 5:17 (NIV)

And may you have the power to understand, as all God's people should, how wide, how long, how high, and how deep his love is.

–EPHESIANS 3:18 (NLT)

Written in the sky

HAVE FAITH

Faith

God keeps promises

My favorite artist is God

Look to the rainbow

abide
IN HIM

Jesus is
the vine

never
apart

Branching out for the Lord

"When I see the rainbow in the clouds, I will remember the eternal covenant between God and every living creature on earth."

—GENESIS 9:16 (NLT)

"I am the vine; you are the branches. Those who abide in me and I in them bear much fruit, because apart from me you can do nothing."

—JOHN 15:5 (NRSVUE)

God is in this with me

THROUGH THE FIRES

He is still good.

One God

But if not...

Jesus

Higher than

HIS WAYS ARE
THE BEST WAYS

REST
IN
HIS
WISDOM

Not my way
but Yahweh

Only God sees the finish

"If our God whom we serve is able to deliver us from the furnace of blazing fire and out of your hand, O king, let him deliver us. But if not, be it known to you, O king, that we will not serve your gods and we will not worship the golden statue that you have set up."

-DANIEL 3:17-18 (NRSVUE)

For my thoughts are
not your thoughts,
nor are your ways my ways,
says the Lord.

For as the heavens are
higher than the earth,
so are my ways higher
than your ways
and my thoughts
than your thoughts.

—ISAIAH 55:8–9 (NRSVUE)

Wisdom Power Love

Where you go, I go

Hope of the earth

OUR GOD IS AN AWESOME GOD

Come together
& come to Jesus

You will find rest

Lay it at the feet of the Lord

Souled out
to Jesus

Hope of
humble
hearts

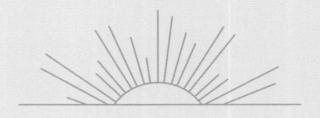

You faithfully answer our prayers with awesome deeds, O God our savior. You are the hope of everyone on earth, even those who sail on distant seas.

-PSALM 65:5 (NLT)

"Come to me, all you who are weary and burdened, and I will give you rest. Take my yoke upon you and learn from me, for I am gentle and humble in heart, and you will find rest for your souls."

—MATTHEW 11:28-29 (NIV)

Blessed

ONLY
FROM
GOD

May I make the Lord smile today

Jehovah Jireh ♥

Look to the Lord

GOD LOVES YOU AND ME

TRUST IN HIS LOVE

LOVE BEYOND MEASURE

LIVE IN GOD & LOVE

God IS Love

'May the LORD bless
you and protect you.

May the LORD smile
on you and be
gracious to you.

May the LORD show
you his favor and
give you his peace.'

—NUMBERS 6:24–26 (NLT)

We know how much God loves us, and we have put our trust in his love.

God is love, and all who live in love live in God, and God lives in them.

–1 JOHN 4:16 (NLT)

soar like
eagles

HE IS
Strong
FOR US

SHAKE OFF
WEARINESS,
TAKE HOLD
OF HIS
STRENGTH

TRUST

wait
&
trust

The struggle is real but so is our God

peace

in His presence

But those who trust
in the Lᴏʀᴅ will find
new strength.

They will soar high on
wings like eagles.

They will run and
not grow weary.

They will walk
and not faint.

—ISAIAH 40:31 (NLT)

You show me the path
of life. In your presence
there is fullness of joy;
in your right hand are
pleasures forevermore.

–PSALM 16:11 (NRSVUE)

LOVE
JOY PEACE
PATIENCE

Such things

BEAR
GOOD
FRUIT

Blessed WITH
the Spirit

THE
FRUIT
OF THE
SPIRIT IS
LOVE, JOY, PEACE
LONGSUFFERING
KINDNESS, GOODNESS
FAITHFULNESS
GENTLENESS
SELF-CONTROL

Be my Storm Stiller

Jesus is my, calm

GOD'S
got this.

Safe through the seas

Praise You in the Storm

But the fruit of the Spirit is love, joy, peace, patience, kindness, goodness, faith, gentleness, and self-control. Against such things there is no law.

-GALATIANS 5:22-23 (WEB)

He stilled the storm to a whisper; the waves of the sea were hushed.

–PSALM 107:29 (NIV)

JESUS

100% GOOD

God
is
so good

Raised on

SWEET TEA

AND

Jesus

Sweeter than honey

Jesus is
my jam

I will follow

faith

LIVE TO MAKE CHRIST KNOWN

Nets of love

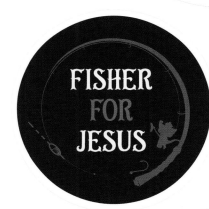

FISHER FOR JESUS

IRRESISTIBLE FAITH

Jesus

**Taste and see that
the Lord is good.**

**Oh, the joys of those
who take refuge in him!**

—PSALM 34:8 (NLT)

"Come, follow me,"
Jesus said, "and I
will send you out
to fish for people."

−MATTHEW 4:19 (NIV)

MY HEART IS SEEN

wholly loved

God only knows

Broken yet beautiful

NEVER ALONE

Stay salty

Remain in Christ

Be who Jesus says you are

Salt Life

Preserve the good

Salty

If our hearts
condemn us, we
know that God is
greater than our
hearts, and he
knows everything.

–1 JOHN 3:20 (NIV)

"You are the salt of the earth. But if the salt loses its saltiness, how can it be made salty again? It is no longer good for anything, except to be thrown out and trampled underfoot."

—MATTHEW 5:13 (NIV)

LOVE
NEVER GIVES UP

LOST & FOUND

100th
sheep

LEAD ON,
GOOD
SHEPHERD

99
for 1

SWEET
Surrender

TRUST
IN THE LORD WITH
ALL YOUR
HEART

TRUST

Straight paths when we walk with God →

walk with God

YOUR
FATHER
KNOWS
BEST

Lean on Him

Jesus

"For the Son of Man has come to save that which was lost. What do you think about this? A man has one hundred sheep and one of them is lost. Will he not leave the ninety-nine and go to the mountains to look for that one lost sheep?"

—MATTHEW 18:11-12 (NLV)

Trust in the LORD with all your heart

and lean not on your own understanding;

in all your ways submit to him,

and he will make your paths straight.

–PROVERBS 3:5-6 (NIV)

GRACE

changes everything

SINS *away*

CLEANSED *in CHRIST*

NOT PERFECT
just forgiven

THE *forgives* US *our sins*

Mighty To Save

He's never gonna let you down

expect miracles

(water) walk by Faith

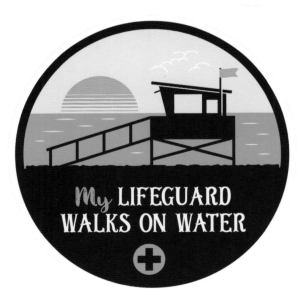

My LIFEGUARD WALKS ON WATER

If we claim we have no sin,
we are only fooling ourselves
and not living in the truth.
But if we confess our sins
to him, he is faithful and
just to forgive us our sins
and to cleanse us from
all wickedness.

-1 JOHN 1:8-9 (NLT)

Meanwhile, the disciples were in trouble far away from land, for a strong wind had risen, and they were fighting heavy waves. About three o'clock in the morning Jesus came toward them, walking on the water.

—MATTHEW 14:24-25 (NLT)

Ask – Seek – Knock

Pray it
believe it
receive it

All good gifts come from above

He's a good, good Father

saved

I'm a whosoever

FOR GOD So Loved THE WORLD

JOHN 3:16

SO LOVED

"Ask, and it will be given you. Seek, and you will find. Knock, and it will be opened for you. For everyone who asks receives. He who seeks finds. To him who knocks it will be opened."

—MATTHEW 7:7-8 (WEB)

For God so loved
the world, that he gave
his only begotten Son,
that whosoever believeth
in him should not perish,
but have everlasting life.
For God sent not his Son into
the world to condemn the
world; but that the world
through him might be saved.

-JOHN 3:16-17 (KJV)

God loves
baby steps

Your Will
be done

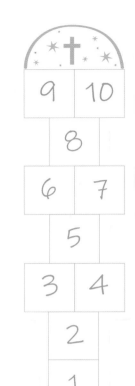

9 10

8

6 7

5

3 4

2

1

small
but strong

Just
Keep
Moving

Do
not
despise
small
beginnings

Have
GODFIDENCE

MAKE HEAVEN CROWDED

Forecast: God reigns

Love on the move

Start spreading the Good News

Beautiful & Good

"Do not despise
these small beginnings,
for the Lᴏʀᴅ rejoices
to see the work begin,
to see the plumb line
in Zerubbabel's hand."

–ZECHARIAH 4:10 (NLT)

How beautiful upon
the mountains are the
feet of the messenger who
announces peace, who brings
good news, who announces
salvation, who says to Zion,
"Your God reigns."

—ISAIAH 52:7 (NRSVUE)

Every day for
FOREVER

Sing to the Lord

MY Heart SINGS

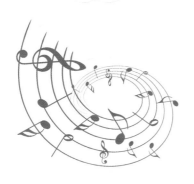

King &
Kingdom,
come

10,000 reasons

Kingdom come

see the **GOOD**, be the **GOOD**

The Lord's been good to me

DON'T **Stop** believing

Gotta have faith

I will exalt you,
my God and King,

and praise your name
forever and ever.

I will praise you
every day;

yes, I will praise
you forever.

—PSALM 145:1-2 (NLT)

Yet I am confident I will see the LORD's goodness

while I am here in the land of the living.

-PSALM 27:13 (NLT)

Wait.

on God

For everything there is a season

His timing is perfect

Hope *does not disappoint*

Our Hope Lives

CHANGE OUR HEARTS

God's love in my heart, coffee in my hands

Holy Spirit, you are welcome here

God has made everything
beautiful for its own time.
He has planted eternity in
the human heart, but even
so, people cannot see the
whole scope of God's work
from beginning to end.

−ECCLESIASTES 3:11 (NLT)

We will not be
disappointed by this
hope. God has given
us the Holy Spirit.
And the Holy Spirit
has put God's love
in our hearts.

—ROMANS 5:5 (WE)

my happy place

is in the Son

I'm not home yet

Set YOUR mind ON things ABOVE

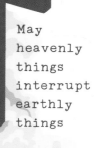

May heavenly things interrupt earthly things

BUT FIRST, Jesus

trust

Open heart,
Jesus hands
& feet

Faith like a child

Believe

Everything
is possible with God

If then you were raised together with Christ, seek the things that are above, where Christ is, seated on the right hand of God. Set your mind on the things that are above, not on the things that are on the earth.

-COLOSSIANS 3:1-2 (WEB)

"Truly I tell you, whoever does not receive the kingdom of God as a little child will never enter it."

—LUKE 18:17 (NRSVUE)

Perseverance - Character - Hope

I CAN
DO ALL
THIS

Glory
in the
sufferings

He has overcome

Consider it all

JOY

For
the
Good

According to His purpose

BEAUTY FROM ASHES

TRUST IN THE LORD
WITH ALL YOUR HEART

God's not done yet

jesus

My brothers and sisters, whenever you face various trials, consider it all joy, because you know that the testing of your faith produces endurance. And let endurance complete its work, so that you may be complete and whole, lacking in nothing.

−James 1:2−4 (NRSVue)

And we know that in all things God works for the good of those who love him, who have been called according to his purpose.

-ROMANS 8:28 (NIV)

His Grace is Enough

NOT FOR ME, BUT FOR HIM

Saved BY Grace

MAKE JESUS a Part of Every DAY

grace

Rise up & pray

MORNING BY MORNING MORNING BY MORNING

THIS IS THE DAY

IN THE MORNING WHEN I RISE, GIVE ME

Jesus

For by grace you have
been saved through faith,
and this is not your own doing;
it is the gift of God—not the
result of works, so that
no one may boast.

—EPHESIANS 2:8–9 (NRSVUE)

The steadfast love of
the LORD never ceases, his
mercies never come to an end;
they are new every morning;
great is your faithfulness.

–LAMENTATIONS 3:22–23 (NRSVUE)

Made in His image

child of God

I AM WHO you SAY I AM

Loved · Created · Chosen · Saved

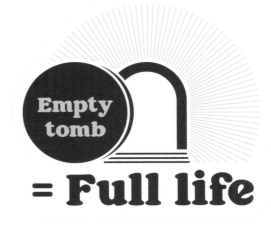

Empty tomb = Full life

Just As He Said

Indeed

So God created humans in his image, in the image of God he created them.

—GENESIS 1:27A (NRSVUE)

But the angel said,
"Don't be alarmed.
You are looking for
Jesus of Nazareth,
who was crucified.
He isn't here!
He is risen
from the dead!"

—MARK 16:6A (NLT)

Mighty to Save

from: Jesus

HIS
NAME
IS
WONDERFUL

PEACE

Jesus is King

JESUS
EVERYTHING

Catch God's hope

Son Protection Factor 100

confident in the Spirit

peace out, peace within

growing in joy

TRUST IN HIS PROTECTION

For a child is born to us.
A son is given to us;
and the government will
be on his shoulders.

His name will be called
Wonderful Counselor, Mighty
God, Everlasting Father,
Prince of Peace.

—ISAIAH 9:6 (WEB)

I pray that God, the source of hope, will fill you completely with joy and peace because you trust in him. Then you will overflow with confident hope through the power of the Holy Spirit.

-ROMANS 15:13 (NLT)

Sticker Inspirations: Praise and Promises to Remind You of God's Love
Copyright © 2025 by Hollan Publishing. All rights reserved. Printed in China.
No part of this book may be used or reproduced in any manner whatsoever without
written permission except in the case of reprints in the context of reviews.

Andrews McMeel Publishing
a division of Andrews McMeel Universal
1130 Walnut Street, Kansas City, Missouri 64106

www.andrewsmcmeel.com

25 26 27 28 29 RLP 10 9 8 7 6 5 4 3 2 1

ISBN: 978-1-5248-9508-2

Scripture quotations marked NIV are taken from THE HOLY BIBLE, NEW INTERNATIONAL VERSION®,
NIV® Copyright ©1973, 1978, 1984, 2011 by Biblica, Inc.® Used by permission. All rights reserved worldwide.

Scripture quotations marked NLT are taken from Holy Bible, New Living Translation,
copyright © 1996, 2004, 2015 by Tyndale House Foundation.
Used by permission of Tyndale House Publishers, Inc., Carol Stream, Illinois 60188.
All rights reserved.

Scripture quotations marked NLV are taken from the New Life Version, copyright © 1969 and 2003.
Used by permission of Barbour Publishing, Inc., Uhrichsville, Ohio 44683.
All rights reserved.

Scripture quotations marked NRSVUE are taken from the New Revised Standard Version Updated Edition.
Copyright © 2021 National Council of Churches of Christ in the United States of America. Used by permission.
All rights reserved worldwide.

Scripture quotations marked WE are taken from THE JESUS BOOK—The Bible in Worldwide English.
Copyright © 1969, 1971, 1996, 1998 by SOON Educational Publications, Willington, Derby,
DE65 6BN, England. Used by permission.

The King James Version (KJV) and World English Bible (WEB) are in the Public Domain.

Designer: Melissa Gerber
Editor: Jennifer Leight
Production Editor: Julie Railsback
Production Manager: Tamara Haus
Illustrations used under license from Shutterstock

ATTENTION: SCHOOLS AND BUSINESSES
Andrews McMeel books are available at quantity discounts with bulk purchase for
educational, business, or sales promotional use. For information, please e-mail the
Andrews McMeel Publishing Special Sales Department: sales@amuniversal.com.

For the Good

GOD'S got this.

Thy Will be Done

HAVE FAITH

faith

Jesus is my calm

For the Good

TRUST IN THE LORD WITH ALL YOUR HEART

Thy Will be Done

HE HAS A PLAN I HAVE A PURPOSE

faith

Faithful Servant